"*Everything finished and happened once, back in the Dreamtime.*
We live in eternity now."

First published by Beyond Images, 2000
PO Box 1457 Camberwell East 3126
Melbourne Victoria Australia

Photographs copyright © John Kirk, 2000
Poems copyright © Mark O'Connor, 2000

Design by Ian Dalton and Associates Pty Ltd
Melbourne Victoria Australia

Printed in China by Everbest Printing Co Ltd

National Library of Australia
Cataloguing~in~Publication Data

O'Connor, Mark, 1945 ~.
The forever lands : Australia's Northern Territory.

ISBN 0 646 39609 9.

1. Northern Territory ~ Pictorial works.
2. Northern Territory ~ Poetry.
I. Kirk, John, 1949~. II. Title.

919.429

www.beyondimages.com.au
www.olympicpoet.com   www.australianpoet.com

THE FOREVER LANDS

Australia's Northern Territory in words and images by

Mark O'Connor & John Kirk

Beyond Images

FOREWORD

Mark O'Connor is all green and gold, as befits our
Olympic poet. He is a conservationist with a scientific
muse, yet he has the polished verbal gold of a classicist.

John Kirk's colours are the blues, reds, greens, and
yellows of Australia's monsoonal north and of the desert
centre. He is a truly remarkable photographic artist.
Readers will surely be amazed at how the land glows and
asserts itself in his images. Even the Aboriginal lightning
spirit Nemargon has yielded to patience and let himself be
photographed live, in one of his millisecond existences.

This is not one of those books where the works of
different types of artists face each other on alternate
pages. The two authors have worked together closely
in the field as on the page. The result is an exceptional col-
laboration of word-imagery and of pictorial imagery
~ the two uniting to create a unique sense of that three-
quarters of our continent which nature has set aside
for mystic poetry.

Les Murray

"*Sand hushes the spinifex aisles*
in a scabbard of wind rustle"

CONTENTS

"*Look up: a rock seems to bat*
                    the swift-pitching clouds"

"Sun bright, air so thin
you scarcely know if you are hot or cold."

FINKE RIVER

The thin pool reflects

a cliff face so sheer and red

kneeling to drink gives you vertigo.

Sun bright, air so thin

you scarcely know if you are hot or cold.

On this high raft of dreaming-plane

your heart catches up with your timetable.

Here and there slips of green

undulled by drought and frost.

This place of rocks and heroic herbs

has a serpenty feel, like Greece

in the rubble beside broken columns

where you crunch on vanished empires

among prickles and scorpions of today.

Monster-filled gorges and dry-sand rivers

Ulysses might have met

if he'd carried his oar far enough.

In delicious cold

at noon on a plain in tropical sun,

you walk soft banks of fines,

long shoals of rubble and half rounded gibber,

bones of a continent mouldering down.

The Finke waits, a river in dry storage,

each ripple and shoalbank preserved

with its foam-chewing boulders

and the deep hole sculpted around a tree bole

from that last flood

~ which may not have been so long ago

though you'd die waiting for it.

A rich land to seed-cracking birds

and fire-proof reptiles,

where honey comes from ants.

How the birds of the air throng in this place

so sure of themselves and their tribes!

"Luckier headwaters...
that hear a rumour of rivers towards a sea."

LOST RIVER

(EXTRACT FROM 'DOT PAINTINGS')

Residual, the Finke is a worm

looping into the desert

whose breath will destroy it.

This river that never meets sea or lake

casts doubt on all others.

Does the Rhine merely muddle to the North Sea?

Long stinging-cells stretch to each patch of green,

to each sometime source,

each rockface known at uncertain times,

or once to have poured sweet rain

in ephemeral sheets.

Luckier headwaters slip the other way

~ a matter of metres ~

and find channels that know

other channels that hear a rumour of rivers

towards a sea.

*"This river that never meets sea or lake
casts doubt on all others."*

"*A cliff at dusk as orange*
as if roasted in egg yolk."

THE CENTRE

The thought of absent water swirls
in dry throats between gorge walls

~ a land eloquent with shadows of water
cool bird-calls in echoing gorges.

Look up: a rock pillar
seems to bat the swift-pitching clouds.
Look back: a willy-willy tugs at the desert,
cupping up seeds from the plain
to where ghost-gums sprout from ledges.

The Olgas ~ rounded domes
above dry pools, singing
the rounded memory of waters.

A cliff at dusk as orange
as if roasted in egg yolk;
clap of dove wings
exploding out of a sandstone gorge.

Your path is a stony torrent's bed,
like a tank trail; it broadens
to piazzas of crazy paving,
arrives at eight pink-and-charcoal galahs
quietly chawing and cha-ing
in high twigs of a ghost-gum at evening.

"The thought of absent water swirls
in dry throats between gorge walls"

"The Olgas - rounded domes above dry pools,
singing the rounded memory of waters."

ROCK ALTAR

"The Rock swims
in that perfect illumination only possible at night."

Seven giant buses, and two semi-articulated,
in the Ayer's Rock carpark.

All around Uluru the rumble of diesels
forever bringing the people in
to this place that has a name
for a first faint brush with the desert,
long window-rows of people peering out,
in search of a centre in the desert.

You can hear from afar the babble of the Sunset City.
500 people ~ many have switched off their motors
to listen to sounds of the sunset.
They are watching the Rock, and watching each other,
drawn by a color-changing Rock
in company into the desert.

Sun down! A cheer
as the tough stone lights with the fire
it has fought off all day.
The glare that dazzled and tortured
glowing on Uluru's broad flanks
and, beyond, on the bright floating highlands
of tonight's full moon. Now the land dims,
crevice and shadow fade; the Rock swims
in that perfect illumination
only possible at night.

A night-wind writes on the sand,
its brush slowly deepening ripples
to last a week.
Scrawlings of bush rat and skink
have only two texts:
Be humbled by your irrelevance;
Rejoice that the world admits you.
Both texts are the same text.

THE ROCK

The Rock has exits and entrances

womb-shaped vacuoles

birth-caves and spring-caves,

V-shaped notches where life and water flow

like syrup from notched bark.

Dreaming spirals in white ochre

make the Rock's spiral nipples flow

with fresh broods of euros, hopping mice, and yams.

Above that jigsaw rockface

lives a timeless Snake.

It has no need of us or the world.

But it can be sung

~ sung, till water flows from its body

in vast sheets down from the baking top,

the black rivers of Uluru,

long trails of dead algae, to a waterfall

that in rain-time belches a town's water supply

The brief river falls from the Rock

in flawless fluted shoals,

drilling an invisible reservoir,

hectares broad, sand-roofed.

The Rock's lizard-shingles

are flaked by millennial frost.

Spinifex bushes mark the cracks

like hairs in an armpit.

A long plate creaking loose

is the Dreamtime Goanna climbing the Rock

~ one day he will split, leap back.

When he lands astonished on his spine

he will, in an instant, rejoin that Dream

where everything happened

and happens again.

"Above that jigsaw rockface lives a timeless Snake.
It has no need of us or the world."

DINOSAUR DREAMING

(FOR MT STEGOSAURUS)

The Dreamtime was true. These rocks all lived.

The land was alive and convulsing when seas were hot mists.

Its rocks bubbled and frothed.

Now they lie flat, yet sluggishly steep

with the long barrel-bodies of crested reptiles

and the stumpy side-legs of salamanders.

Bumping the clouds along their spines,

breaking the hail with a mindless brow,

~ the first brood of Earth

before she invented cooler blood

and flesh that grew in its own water.

"Now they lie flat, yet sluggishly steep
with the long barrel-bodies of crested reptiles."

They had climbed out unknowing.

The mild air, the sliding rivers

turned them to stone.

Pygmy brontosaurids grazed on their sleeping flanks,

the long necks moving

and small things suckling

in a pouch of volcanic tundra

on a snowy raft that drifted round the Pole.

Denting a crustplate that wobbled

over the molten-iron belly, they returned

with boiling lakes on their heads.

The monsters count moons by the million

and the watery suns by day.

The cold ocean of air has invaded them surely

cracking their blood into crystals;

and that subtle and terrible fluid, the water . . .

They are not fooled by summers

or the faint warmth of forest fires.

They hold the valleys between their paws

grimly relenting; or butt back the sand-swell,

flicking its spume from rigid tail bones.

When the sun grows huge, when the Warm has begun,

and the forests boil off their sides like mist

~ then they will shiver

ridging their scale-backs against the stars,

unwinding their tracks all over the Dreamtime

their once and now come-alive time.

ABORIGINAL LITERACY

No books, no Recording Angel myth,

but all's noted as it happens;

not a cockateel falls to earth . . .

The sandhill at morning's a soft slate

of scribbled inscriptions.

Primal spirits of bilbi and native cat

contend in an endless epic

printed on pages a day's walk wide,

that appear round your doorstep each dawn,

the Sandhill Times, Dune Gazette,

with curlicue borders of pigeons' feet.

"Friends of the late respectfully advise . . .

that her tracks met and entered

those of Garbung Goanna . . ."

Between spinifex archipelagoes

a snake sails furtively

half drowning in flat heat.

Nature's so sparse

the sand's her logbook

to prove things happen,

and lead her literate dark-skinned people

to juicy steaks of slithering rope meat.

The sand-swimming goanna,

address deciphered,

roasts like a long stunned mullet

your stick has stung.

"The sandhill at morning's a soft slate
of scribbled inscriptions."

THE SILENCE

(ALICE SPRINGS)

Closing the door, you go out

~ indeed out

from the last line of houses

over the ditch for thirty-year floods

treading dry sand from an ancient ocean

~ fluent signature of a passing snake

the night closing in as ever

and the rock wallabies entering it

~ truck-roar and horns in the distance

like some loud-voiced bird with two notes

that repeats its nothing forever.

Sand hushes the spinifex aisles

in a scabbard of wind-rustle.

"Spinifex
    ~ tussocks you once thought uniform and now think random."

The big roos, like grey mobile spirits

among self-toned stones

observe you from cover.

Motor noise falls away

like a wad pulled from your ears, so thick

there is only silence, the lack.

You are walking small gaps,

and maps, of bare soil between spinifex

~ tussocks you once thought uniform

and now think random

feeling the soft rush of sand between toes

watching for trip-stone or stub-root,

an endless fitting of bare feet to country.

Alice, the sea city, sleeps under its cliffs

in its dry bay, glimpsed through dunes

like Baia's marbles through the wave.

A hundred metres in ~

glance back through a line of shrubs

and the low, busy city is gone,

vanished into the bush like Burke and Wills

and a cool breeze comes,

and gives you back your senses.

"*The Todd ... world's oldest fossil riverbed*
surviving its waters."

AND SOMETIMES WET...

(FROM 'DOT PAINTINGS')

Unliveable heat.

The Todd, a river baked with age

in its earth-oven of burning stones,

world's oldest fossil riverbed

surviving its waters

as a trilobite's shell

survives an ocean.

From each shattered range,

the river flows yellow-full and empty;

a canal of sand soaking slowly

into the dry heart.

31

WILD BUDGERIGARS

In the desert pool a scattering skyful
of lime-greens and yellows, no captive blues.

A hawk's shadow passes, distant, lonely;
they pour in, thickening a mulga's branches,
grinding seed-paste from the grasslands;
they dart, flit, flip, flick, sip drops for dough
from a mud-pool two metres long;
plonk hard down on its gruel,
whir up like houseflies from a swat, return;
less flap than buzz, on stumpy wings
riding an invisible flicker,
they pulse through light and heat, absent
and back, in the twitch of a tomcat's paw.
First there are two, then four,
forty, four hundred, three, then none; and again.

DESERT POOL

How to slow their wing beats, squeals,
so the brain can unravel?
Only that giant muddy eye is swift to snatch
each flurr of radiant wings, give each shrill
squawk its millisecond, and its drink.

The cat mews, disconsolate.
Its first slink from cover
has sent these bright ragged troupes,
querulous parliaments of birds,
whirring up out of the pond's clay eye
that shakes, un-blurs, and empties.

Camel and butterfly stagger in
for refreshment
one on the other's nose.

GHOST GUMS

Whitely as stardust, a ghost-gum resists

the day's coarse smear of heat.

Rises by quartzite walls:

white against so orange-red;

a monument, marble arms flung out

impossibly wide and high in a desert;

rock-like among rocks, her waist reflecting

night-frost and noon-sear.

Exultant branchlets upstretch

into solar flares

weeping tresses of springtime green.

The flame robin flirts in her shadow

where the skink hides.

High above, like eye-pupils,

two black dots winging and circling

up in the hot yellow, searching.

How can she rise so assured

when all around is seared and crippled?

~ In certain nooks by invisible soaks or banks

of forgotten rivers under the sand

each under its cloud of tossing green,

a doric column, not gracile, robust.

"*How can she rise so assured*
when all around is seared and crippled?"

"The basin with its watchers is
cool and tranquil."

AT EDITH FALLS

A plain of gray water between giant bluffs.

In the centre a sand bank, deduced

from the man standing on it.

He calls to the girl

who sits hugging her lack of bra.

She dives ~ idling out with a frog kick,

her whiteness dissolving in ripples.

Half asleep I am watching

this tranquil basin where no ducks swim,

I and the other observer,

that line of driftwood

with pine-cone serrations of a tail.

It rides oddly high, bobbing

and fading in scaly ripples.

It turns, revolving as no log could

to point its long barrel at the noise

~ harmless snout of a freshwater croc.

The yellow-beaked honeyeater cries to its friends

of the hawk and the brown egg-snake

that found its nest this year ~ its lament

a small blink in the croc's long afternoon.

It flits between two grevilleas,

darts out, lands briefly at the snout,

and sips. Flies off;

the log churns away

to resurface, pointing.

Later the harmless croc is gone. The girl

swims back,

climbs on the rocks,

and the honeyeater finds its tribe

among golden nectar-dripping cones.

The basin with its watchers is cool

and tranquil, scaly surfaced.

"That line of driftwood
with pine-cone serrations of a tail."

ROCK PAINTINGS

(KATHERINE GORGE)

All day the barges come and go,

bringing folk from Florida, Iceland, China.

The guide explains how paintings were made

of ochre rubbed in with goanna fat.

These figures once hid such truth

boys would take circumcision with stone

to enter their world.

And nobody knows what they mean.

But the Rainbow Serpent winds through them all

over the serpentine gorge.

The Lizard Man and the Kangaroo Woman

have gone hunting. They stand,

coat-of-arms style, each side of the fire;

he with his knees turned out, and huge testicle bag.

A joey peeps from the Woman's pouch, applauds.

They have hung seven herons upon their spit.

And a turtle swings from the Lizard Man's hand.

Above, a vast figure,

arms spread, accepts their gift,

the rest is worn away.

And nobody knows what it means.

No one remembers a thing.

Beside are the Jabiru spirit, two masked beings,

and three with spiky head-dresses, hung

like the herons on a fire.

A thousand years before,

folk leaned a forked tree on this cliff

and rigged a cradle for the artist.

And nobody knows why they did it.

Nobody knows what it means.

"*The Rainbow Serpent winds through them all*
over the serpentine gorge."

TERMITE LANDS

Driving into the nothing,

the road trains and erosion gullies,

the burnt dead-swamp heart

where termite trees are all that grow;

past a biking swagman,

brain-burnt beyond lure of comfort.

Striking through smoky air,

the breath of the burning continent,

a hawk sheds the sun-strike off its wing

slicing up from the leading edge

a wake of cool low-pressure.

Like fire-walkers whose feet would bubble

if they stop, our tyres scorch

down the melting bitumen strip

through air made breathable by speed.

Stop, and you're in the Territory.

"Striking through smoky air,
the breath of the burning continent."

"The coast's dun-green carpet tatters and shreds...
shrinks back to creeks."

FLYING OVER THE TOP END
(SINGAPORE TO BRISBANE FLIGHT)

Dawn is a curve of primal white

so distant it seems straight,

ruled by a continent-sized protractor.

The black land, saucer of chaos,

waits for creating light, for the fire-glow

lit by a screaming torch of parrots.

Clouds marshal in lines for the day,

each pegged to a shadow

in scrub that stipples the hot red soil

lapped by oceans of land-killing salt.

The coast's dun-green carpet tatters and shreds,

worn off from the hills, torn by horned maggots,

shrinks back to creeks.

The plane's shadow stubs itself

on ridges and seams

of a continental weld, bumping

over the dragon-breath plains,

where desert peoples winnow grass seeds,

share honey-ants, living

that perfect democracy whose each citizen

is a Local Member.

Rim-dwellers, we doze and snack,

descending on the wet coast.

ICE AGE FIELDS

Jabiluka plain, a vast lawn of goose-mown grass,
seems an old lake-bed ~ and is, from three months back.
Its harvest, in spike-rush bulbs, exceeds a wheatfield.

Brindled geese and white herons move on it, placid as sheep.
A distant flock rises, revolves, and planes to some new down.

Pelicans cross it on lazy wings, flap, flop, glide
~ taking the beat from their leader.

In Jabiluka Billabong the archer fish hang at the surface,
careless of herons.
Their eye, that can see to shoot a midge,
holds the sky and all its beaks
lightly in fish-eye crystal.

The floodplain bakes to splitting seedful mud
where the Lightning Man will strike his axe.
The Rainbow Serpent, blood-scenting dragon, resplendent
monsoonal air-snake that upswims the rising mist,
swirls hungrily to the fertile smell
of a girl's first blood at puberty,
swilling the land to mud-brick soup
that brims with birth.

The white distant trunks and wet greens
might be English but for the killing heat
~ a wood surrounding a pleasant dale
where knights joust from a line of trees.

This was the Ice Age land of the Yam People
who drew themselves as pregnant tubers
with plump distorted heads and legs
ten millennia since, on a high cold plateau.
That same cold-drought begins
afresh each winter, till the Wet …

"*A vast lawn of goose-mown grass,*
seems an old lake bed..."

"*Newcomers squeeze in shyly, as in church,*
setting up with soft intrusive rustlings."

FEEDING PLAINS ~ MAMUKALA

Magpie geese:

seven black periscopes

in a sea of green wild rice.

Distant grey hummocks:

a flock of brolgas is grazing ~ stalked

from shadows of the hide,

coveys of clickers and twitchers

in hushed dim frenzy

pecking film in and out of boxes,

snapping and feeding.

Newcomers squeeze in shyly,

as in church, setting up

with soft intrusive rustlings.

Miles beyond,

a quiet click of motel-registers;

half a continent further

bureaucrats pause in their tallying,

hum at the rightness of things.

The brolgas take off,

down their bush airstrip

hopping and bumping,

gain speed, till a hop-leap-hop

stalls them up into the air,

a slow, graceful semaphore

wing-beats not blurred.

They rise, revealing graceful extension-legs,

giant cranes clambering massively into the sunset,

their day's business done, and safe

as an updraft floats them back

two kilometres over our heads.

MAGELA FLOODPLAIN AT DAWN

A dazzle licks at the rim of the world,

flame at the edge of tinder;

vast honking of goose horns

like a traffic jam in the dark

then across a slate mirror

the cattle-egret runs to a splash

its coiled neck-javelin at the ready

and the leaf-trotting jacana,

lark of the floodplain,

kicks puddles that bounce on a green lily leaf

like spilt mercury on glass

and the tiny white waterlily fakes

a carpet of English snowdrops

among tropical sedges

in warm reptilian waters.

"And the leaf-trotting jacana
kicks puddles ... like spilt mercury on glass."

"*And the tiny white waterlily fakes*
a carpet of English snowdrops"

"*The sea-eagle's hovering spread*
struggles to jemmy a catfish from water."

JABIRUS AT ANABANGBANG

The jabiru stork is hunting,

is moving his fleshless shanks

red and inert as pipes

hitched to long muscles

under the feathers. He lifts one leg,

now the other, considering, stirring.

His mate runs, ungainly, after the shoals

as they swirl and mill,

confused in mud-shallows,

then pay her toll for escape.

Twin derricks in the swamp

the pair feed from stilts

as others from the air.

The sea-eagle's hovering spread

struggles to jemmy a catfish from water,

jumps and bucks like a tethered kite

as the spined tail still under and beating

twists him ninety degrees from the strike-path;

but the jabiru pair lift with ease

whatever their bludgeon-beaks stun.

Lesser ducks and magpie-geese may dabble

beneath them; and the small heron

keeps his intent bent-necked pose,

a feathered snake waiting to strike;

the file-snake thinks him a branch,

is stung, resists, despairs.

Above, black cockatoos in flight:

their slow archaic wail,

their strange, slack falling asleep

at the end of each downstroke.

"*Derricks in the swamp...*
feed from stilts as others from the air."

"Overpaid conference delegates,
the convention of pelicans."

A QUOKKLE
OF PELICANS

Overpaid conference delegates,

the convention of pelicans, splayfoots,

potbellied, full heads,

waddle together, trading opinions,

chaw over beakfuls of tiddlers.

EGRET STANCES

The egret leans like a notary, invigilates

the bona fides of a lotus clump,

plucks out the frog of error.

~ ~

Two egrets leaning

too much. Each threatens the tuft

beyond his neighbour's.

~ ~

Exposed, frog stares heron in the beak

knowing itself delicious flesh

that will breed if it leaps away.

~ ~

Frog leaps and loses.

By the many eggs

of a few survivors

a species lives, eternal.

"An eye blinks...
surprised only at your surprise."

LOGS

(FROM 'CREAM OF EARTH')

In the mangrove channels you find them,

submerged, flying the flag of two minor branches

over a ton of brown torpedo.

Others cruise roots-up, pushing a crab-claw

of snapped root in your face. You manoeuvre past,

thinking them sea-bound. Swirling back that night

with high tide, they crash past your boat.

Then you see them for weeks, the same ones going and coming:

Mad Maurie, Racing Ray . . .

Approaching, you learn to keep hands in. A touch

on that mud-greased hardwood, the prow swings

and jams, pulping fingers to cray-meat.

You learn each one's profile, judge dangers,

you think, to a thumb's width; till you find they pulse

between two states: Hulking Harry on Mondays and Wednesdays

inverts to Jinxing Gillian;

Pretty Polly's sometimes Deadly Dan.

"In the mangrove channels you find them,
submerged ... over a ton of brown torpedo."

IBIS FLAPPING

The kingfisher flits, glinting

turquoise over the crocodile swamp.

~ For adventure, choose the mild crocodile

not the tiger. He'll sharpen your senses,

make you inspect each log;

a gentleman killer, stalks you

on ground of your choosing. Stay away

and you need never play.

Yet the croc scores

~ an ibis flaps

as the broken leg pulls under.

No fantasies of digging thumbs

in that soft under-belly

of half-inch armour.

Surfacing

slowly

so slowly

a serrated tail breaks water

like six autumn leaves raked at an angle.

An eye blinks, perfect

as the yellow waterlily flower,

surprised only at your surprise.

He won't strike

till he's got the range. Then broad

tail thrusting, rush

of the squat webbed feet, a gecko

launched at a moth,

and you turn, dream-slow,

to push uphill through sinking mud

~ an ibis flapping.

"*A gentleman killer, stalks you
on ground of your choosing.*"

"Rock bobs in not quite the same place,
a croc drifting across the bay at dusk."

CROCODILE ZEN

A sea like after loving, so warm
and flat each wave
exhausts it for minutes.
Rock bobs in not quite the same place,
a croc drifting across the bay at dusk.
The sun goes down in fiery yellow
and all the world is as it must.

Tonight you will dream
the mating of crocodiles,
armoured belly to belly
churning thick ooze
in a perfect weightless bed.

Breeze-patterned bay, evening peace,
scatter of fish-jumps,
random feeding.

"*The sun goes down in fiery yellow
and all the world is as it must.*"

REFLECTION

A jungle pool keeps bouncing the sky

in shimmering panes through the leaves

leaping among the quandong fruit.

~~

Impossibly, lightly

a butterfly's shadow taps

the pond's top, from below.

~~

Deep in the billabong

a mirrored hawk swoops up

on a flock of whistling-duck

that scatter, flee

up to the surface.

"*Impossibly, lightly a butterfly's shadow*
taps the pond's top from below."

NEMARGON, THE LIGHTNING GRASSHOPPER

To make thunder

says Nemargon the Lightning Man,

strike your axe against rock.

To make lightning

axe on axe

flint-head to flint-head

till the pure spark leaps.

For a Gunumelung storm

you cannot have too many axes, or arms.

The Lightning God wears

a girdle of axe-heads;

he sends out his messenger, the six-armed

lightning grasshopper, proclaiming

reds and orange and the sharp blue

between stricken stones

The grasshopper chirrups,

in two or three places,

his stridulent song of Nemargon

whetting his stone. One vibrant messenger

to each valley. Pluck him

out of his chosen tussock

~ you grasp the cyclone in your hand.

"Axe on axe
flint-head to flint-head till the pure spark leaps."

"*The six-armed lightning grasshoppers,*
proclaiming reds and orange and the sharp blue."

"The rain's barrage moves in, gets our range,
... drops hiss on rocks still hot to touch."

ON THE ESCARPMENT

The draft swirls up with eucalyptus smell,
heated by rocks where the ants dance
too quick for the eye.
The late-day warmth is strange and hard
like an embrace from Earth itself.

To watch such power from such height
is millionaire stuff in the cities.
Our perched cathedral-barn of a cave came free
with the bones and paint of millennial occupants,
and the ochred hand of a child,
long since grown warrior or mother.

A sheer view of clouds and monsoonal plain
that could pull from your lungs
the hooting whistle of a kite.

The rain's barrage moves in, gets our range;
frogs crank up; drops hiss
on rocks still hot to touch.

We watch the monsoon's first plumblines drop
and the months begin
of the lightning's miles-in-a-millisecond.

Pseudo-solid water
bouncing down sandstone strata
takes false shapes, persistent, ephemeral;
molten glass, fused and blown;
its loose avalanche stumbles
down a rock-valley worn to curves
of this afternoon's currents
and those since the last Ice Age,
as the rock that water made
water now slowly disassembles.

Sparklets of sun through softening rain.
The wreck of a storm staggers
away from the sunset
blazing and howling into the East.

"As the valley clears, obscures, half-clears
like a lens pulled in and out of focus."

FEBRUARY STORMS

It's the green Wet
~ warm spit between down-drubs.
Where else can you laugh
so much water off your back?

Yam vines
half-shot from tubers, now begin
to put substance back. The year
is floral, confident. The kestrel cries
that half the Wet is gone.

The paperbark blooms now
between too much and too little water;
its white brushes smelling of honey and meat
enthrall the flies.

Your noon siesta floats
from unbearable sweat and lassitude
to cool passionate thunder
~ a swift rise of yeasting cloud-cells;

cold grit in the eye as the gust-front swirls,
shrouds ~ vanishes, and then the rain.

That first sharp spray~what else but spit, or seed?
And the cool that follows, the end of some broil
between sky and earth
~ birds the urgent messengers
of its start and end,
the downpour its fertile resolution,
as the valley clears, obscures, half-clears
like a lens pulled in and out of focus.

Blissful too, the cool evenings after rain
in which perhaps you've showered.

"*The paperbark blooms now between too much*
and too little water."

"*Random though the world may be*
the viscosity of water's right."

THE VISCOSITY OF WATER

Random though the world may be

the viscosity of water's right.

If more, it would strain

molasses-thick, glacier-slow.

If less, it would skip like a squirrel,

streams flee their beds in a heartbeat,

currents zip like electrons

from high point to low

till trout were unthinkable,

Boats would be curved to surf a flash-flood.

No punts, no skiffs,

no rowing eights or deep dinghies

would dent the meniscus of smooth-brimming streams

whose mouth is lower than their source.

Though families watching

from the rafts of verandahs

a glug of slow-draining khaki over crops, cars, cattle

would wish this fluid had no viscosity,

I cannot unwish the joy of white waterfalls

whose standing wave is shaped like glass,

of the sculptures of water and rock,

water-sculpted rock, rock-sculpted water,

or a trunk as fluid-shaped as the rock;

or rivers rising softly

as sleepers nudged by vague sense of the dawn,

seeping from nowhere,

from some gland of the continent;

or those sandstone creeks

that rise and fall each hour

as rain pelts or pats,

charting a cliff's run-off as neatly

as tank-rungs do for a tin roof;

or those puckering spurts a pool makes

as it nears some lip of unstandable gravity

where each departing wave sucks on the next

to drum, soft shrapnel, on white distant rocks;

let us be grateful even

for dew-ponds and peat-swamps,

spongy tussock and tadpole pool,

papyrus and reedy back-water;

for tarn, loch, mere, meander,

channel, billabong ~ wherever

the swift flighty fluid lets us treat it as a plain;

for this Kakadu swamp just filling

that fell as a thousand bouncing beads

in today's allotted storm,

floating the withered grass;

for the blessings of loose water

everywhere visible/invisible

free-running on rock and leaf

unbondable supreme escapist, lucid

shape-slipper, skipping sea-bound

past the dam's compound or the crooked detour

of a town's hollow kidneys;

for water taking its time, unhurried

through sand-shoals and rock-riffles,

utterly present while it is present,

thrusting up sticks and bodies

with a push as heavy as the hole each makes,

never skimping its present duty on plea

of haste to the salt;

grateful above all for the progress of rivers

which, facing no obstacles, yet make their own time

signing the plains with stately meanders,

descending the slopes in a wide wilful slalom,

as though in love with the land

unwilling to part from the Earth.

"Descending the slopes in a wide wilful slalom,
as though in love with the land."

79

"*The wreck of a storm staggers*
away from the sunset."

81

THE GRASSHOPPER MAN

~ Nemargon the thunderer
whetting his axe
till his storm will crash,
gusting inside the overhang.

His groin is shaped insectwise
like a clutch of axeheads,
stone prisms jangling together.
Antenna'd, sometimes breasted,
he grinds the stone axes on his knees
till shivers of lightning leap
from clashed genitals.

Barginj his wife, the Lightning Woman,
sprawls beside, in a birth pose;
her groin is a slot, an open mouth
fervently pouring out life;

strained inner sinews
binding its purse together.
Her head a skull,
whose round sockets mimic breasts.

In the Wet, cool season for birth,
the open cave trembles, walled
by blue electric sheets.
A spidery hand reaches out in white
to touch her electric husband.

A Gagadju woman squats in birth,
triangular breasts tilt ripely to each side.
Namandi the evil one squats, legs splayed,
ochre-red, with a dilly bag of harms
for the mother's heart, lungs, kidney.

Never touch the late-Spring grasshopper,
messenger and insect-child of Nemargon
~ his blue and orange mandibles will sting
like snakes, his bitter whirr explode.

"Nemargon the thunderer whetting his axe
till his storm will crash ..."

A CAVE

is split-level living:

with verandahed overhang,

sun-roof on top

and a cooler cabin under

where meat keeps for two more meals.

Upstairs on the roof, you sit at dawn

scanning the plain for game,

talking strategy with men whose speed was famous once.

And later the kids will climb up there

counting which goose-mobs flew which way.

Just below should be a deep-flowing river

with nets spread for ducks

and a far bank where the Others come to trade,

kill, kidnap.

In an age of stone

the sacred cave and the ziggurat are one.

Its roof is to light fires on

and signal the hunters home at dark.

Happy she

who sits on the roof of her cave

to see the game scattered across the plain

for tomorrow's meal, and next year's, and all

of the grandchildren's lives

~ she who can sit on the roof of her world

watching the floodplain fill with eels,

the green margin springing with grass

at the waters' retreat, knowing the causes of things,

watching the tall line of trees

by the channel that never dries;

the Goanna Dreaming site

where fresh goannas are bred inexhaustible

to roast in their scales in the ashes;

and, westward, the Maker Serpent cave

where the baby-spirits wait

to re-enter the bodies of women ~ guarded

by the snake family living there.

Happy he who can see, far off, the spot where, a boy,

he killed his first wallaby;

and, revolving all the spots where he might die,

knows how his bones will be broken,

cleaned, and tied in dilly bags

in the burial niche,

while elsewhere his spirit returns

~ a hundred times, then another hundred.

"A cave
is split level living."

LOST ART

~ That slow gentle shock

as you enter a cave

praising yourself to have found its refuge,

then that first sense, half chill on your spine,

at how the dark splotches run together

till the faint reddish stain

might just be a thylacine,

could not be an accident.

NEAR UBIRR

Entering a cave you shout to the bones

within it, mothers, grandfathers, uncles,

saying who comes and not to hurt

the stranger who stands with you.

A painting 10,000 years old

impossibly high on the cave-roof

~ old people say a Mimi did it,

but the pile of fallen rocks

is a vanished ledge.

The dancing figures are elongate

with arms, cocks, legs asplay;

horizontal, head down, or upright

like an aerial dogfight.

The giant barramundi, half human,

half spirit, are the oldtime size

that took two warriors to carry

before the creeks were netted.

This people through ages

never brought in a log to sit on

or knocked the sharp edges from a stone bench,

yet will carefully, daily, sift

pebbles from a patch of sand to sit.

Dusk: and the cave is astir with spirits:

thin Mimi spirits washed out of the cracks

by evening wind or the smell of meat.

At the silent whirr of a small black bat

the screw-palms toss their tousled vanes;

and the flying fox, that human face with wings

drifts past on blacked-out velvet.

A gecko on the sandy track outside

flurries and flees,

blood-warm beneath your sandal.

"*Dusk: and the cave is astir with spirits:*
thin Mimi spirits washed out of the cracks."

"This my land,
all these mine."

AT UBIRR OVERHANG

The wall is a harvest festival:
tortoise, possum, wallaby, goanna,
a shoal of giant barramundi
turning flank-on to the spear
grubbing nose-down for a hook
in rich floodplain detritus.

Golden as dreams,
a long necked tortoise and a salmon-catfish
swim near the overhang's ceiling. Each whisker,
lovingly trapped in ochre, asking
an extra catch.

In X-Ray art
the goanna's drawn flensing-style
with intricate knowledge of cuts and steaks;
the wallaby, a muscled
bunch of gizzards, meat.

In the roof's miraculous thicket of fish
eel-heads peer out of garfish spines
on older lungfish scales.
Prawn and water-monitor thicken
that shoal from a thousand years of net.
A stencilled hand clamps onto
a fat catfish carapace,
"This my land, all these mine".

PORTRAIT BY THE ARTIST

(NOURLANGIE CAVES, KAKADU)

Lying up here since forever
the Barramundi People watched the Wet each year
bring fat shoals almost to their feet,
and in the mud, like great grey living stones
the salt-water crocodiles come up to take
their yearly chance of tribute.
At intervals in the thunder's play
when a curtain mistily went up,
members trapped in the smaller cave
could wave.

For a tribe of twenty
there's nothing statistical
about births, marriages, deaths.
Women with swollen, dripping breasts,
were an ochred hope and omen
for a tribe filling that niche
between too many and none left
for ten thousand years

till there was only Barramundi Charlie
camping here in the last weeks of his life,
~ drawing these monsters on the walls, placating
Mimi spirits so thin they need only tap
to have rocks take them in. Re-claiming
the childhood world he drew round him like a blanket,
with figures of increase for his vanishing
syphilitic, shot and drunken tribe

~ an old man, despised,
soon to be famous,
renewing the world with the ordinary skills,
while his body rotted here
where religion and increase
had worked for millennia.

"*The Barramundi People watched the Wet each year*
bring fat shoals almost to their feet."

"And Barramundi Charlie came here with his Reckitt's blue
painting his people back into the country."

NOURLANGIE CAVE AT NIGHT

~ Utter stillness of warm air among rocks
as if ancestors held their breath.

Each niche has held its dilly bag
of cracked thigh-bones, feared and untouchable
till the brutal four-wheel drives.

And Barramundi Charlie came here with his Reckitt's Blue
painting his people back into the country
under the great faulted cliffs of Arnhem Land
where the line was held, and the farms stopped short.

From dry walls the Rainbow Serpent thunders:
without her lashing explosion
no life, no food, no worshipper.

The Lightning Man and Woman have no mouth,
~ their speech is in the spark
that leaps from stricken stones.

Timeless,
primal Wallaby takes the spear in his lung,
drips blood and baby-making fat.

A horseshoe bat loops softly past my ears,
harmless unless to moths;
the vast bulk of stone a blackness
and comfort from tomorrow's sun.

A python, heat-seeker, lazily unwinds
from the blinding heat of day,
nosing out into the blood-warm night.
The crisp chill before dawn will turn it murderous.

"*A dazzle licks at the rim of the world,*
flame at the edge of tinder."

THE MUD FOREST

A forest, like dipped litmus-paper, maps

the lines of fresh and salt. To flee the tides,

trees have climbed, roots and all, out of the mud,

forming the mangel, the dark man-grove.

Ceriops trunks are the axe-handle forests,

their pale wood, bark-stripped,

with a club of buttress at the base.

Bruguiera fills the ground with knee-cap roots.

Rhizopora's elbow-roots jag upward, then drive down

like infants tucking in at meals

~ its cane-work thicket trails a shoal

of diminishing loops down stream.

Trunks competitive as pines, the neat shafts

spring-lifting from a shoal of hoops

soar upwards in the wind: each twists

in its tube of allotted space, and sun.

Below they lace roots, hold up

the forest where a single tree would fall,

their leafy sails spread taut. To blow them down

the wind must blow the land away.

"*To flee the tides,*
trees have climbed ... out of the mud."

"To blow them down
the wind must blow the land away."

MOON OVER MINDIL BEACH

The moon rises, baseball round,

big as Africa

up over the sea's rim,

pock-marked, full.

Its straight course torn in a circle

by rough pull of Earth.

No passion on earth like the tug of these two

that can never tire of pulling,

never slip their total hold.

Judo-wrestlers, fixed

to each other's lapels,

whirled on a mutual pivot.

Indifferent to shooting stars

or to encrusting empires

each feels only the tug that comes

from the other's dead centre.

K-Marts and craters will ravage them both

without putting pause to this dance

where one hefts the other round its hip

~ thirty diameters away.

"The moon rises, baseball round...
up over the sea's rim, pock-marked, full."

DRAWN IN SAND

(FROM 'DOT PAINTINGS')

In dreams you return

to that cluster of nations whose abstract art

is not distinguished from their maps, not broken

to the small world inside an artist's head

a precise universe built

from a blizzard of dots

~ no straight meaningless roads,

every path a contour, truth, and tucker

~ Its river-courses

dry statements of intent, conditional,

blossoming rarely

with brown loops of clayey water.

Australia shams dry,

turning outward its reptile surface;

blues and greens reflect

fluid everywhere under.

As though the land swirled and flowed

from certain sites of Increase;

soaks, and scrapes and shallow holes in rock

are the timeless Dreaming spirals

from which fresh litters flowed and flow

as milk weeps from an echidna's ductless udder

richly among the spines.

~ ~

Everything finished and happened once, back in the Dreamtime.

We live in eternity now.

"A precise universe built from a blizzard of dots."

ACKNOWLEDGEMENTS

John Kirk would like to acknowledge the following for their support and assistance in making the publication of this unique book possible.

Ian Dalton and Associates (Melanie Clark, Jeff Christesen, and Harry Howard) for their creative effort in designing this book.

To Jack Coppinger and Mike Chuk (former Park Rangers, Conservation Commission NT) for sharing their great passion for the land of Central Australia. John would also like to acknowledge Big Bill Neidjie and members of his family for sharing with us their place in Kakadu. He is very grateful for the friendship and professional advice received from fellow photographer Peter Jarver of Thunderhead Photographics. To John Clarke and the Duckpond in Adelaide, many thanks for providing film and processing for the 1990 expedition into Kakadu. Finally, John thanks the many friends in Darwin who introduced him to the wonders of Kakadu and the Top End and who demonstrated considerable understanding when he made hasty departures to photograph the awesome spectacle of Darwin's tropical storms.

Mark O'Connor would like to acknowledge that the writing of these poems was assisted by fellowships from the Literature Fund/Board of the Australia Council in 1989, and 2000, and by a lesser grant in 1986. He is grateful to John Leonard for editorial advice; and to David Headon and Trevor James for arranging two 3-month residencies for him (jointly supported by the Australia Council and the University of the Northern Territory). Also to various staff-members of the University, including the anthropologist Mark de Graaf who introduced him to the Western Desert. Further poems emerged during a year as the Australian National University's H.C. Coombs Creative Arts Fellow in 1999, and stimulated by the company of Rhys Jones, Geoffrey Hope, and others.

Also to the Northern Territory Conservation Commission for taking him to the Coburg Peninsula; and to those who introduced him to many parts of the Top End and Centre, including Tony and Ro Edwards, Bill Neidjie and members of his family, John Kirk, Peter and Debbie Jarver, Rod Moss, Graham Calley, Sarah Amies, Marilyn Ball, Elizabeth Desailly, Terry Hartney, David and Jean Farquhar, Kim and Valerie Rowe, David Morton, Greg Miles, Jane Moore, Mike and Ilse O'Ferrall, Peter Adsett and Stella Huttlestone.

John and Mark are most grateful to the Northern Territory Government Tourist Bureau, to Qantas, Budget Rent a Car, C'Est Ca, A.C.F., and William Mora Galleries for collectively sponsoring themselves, photographer Peter Jarver, musician Christie Cooney, and artist Peter Adsett on a expedition to Kakadu in 1989.

Both John and Mark also acknowledge the generosity of the various Aboriginal communities in the Northern Territory who have opened up many of their sacred sites to share with the public. The photographs of Aboriginal art presented in this book are from these open sites. The photographs have been made according to the rules applying at the time and with permission from the Aboriginal owners and authorities.

THE IMAGES